T0154028

SEDER IN MOTION

A Haggadah to Move Body and Soul

BY Rabbi Ron Isaacs AND Dr. Leora Isaacs
ILLUSTRATED BY Martin Wickstrom

BEHRMAN HOUSE
www.behrmanhouse.com

FOR MOREY AND RUTHIE EDELMAN

THANKS FOR 30 YEARS OF GREAT SEDERS.
OUR WISH: NEXT YEAR WITH THE EDELMANS!

—Ron and Leora Isaacs

Editorial Consultants: Judith Sandman, Rabbi Josh Stanton, Abe Weschler
Mindfulness Consultant: Joanie Terrizzi
Editorial Development: Dr. Deborah Fripp
Project Manager: Terry S. Kaye
Art Director: Ann Koffsky
Design: Zatar Creative

Copyright © 2021 Ron Isaacs and Leora Isaacs

Art copyright © 2021 Behrman House, Inc.
Millburn, New Jersey

www.behrmanhouse.com

ISBN-13: 978-1-68115-061-1

Printed in the United States of America

LIBRARY OF CONGRESS CATALOGING-IN-PUBLICATION DATA

Names: Isaacs, Ron, author. | Isaacs, Leora W., author. | Wickstrom,
  Martin, illustrator.
Title: Seder in motion : a Haggadah to move body and soul / by Rabbi Ron
  Isaacs and Dr. Leora Isaacs ; art by Martin Wickstrom.
Other titles: Haggadah. Selections.
Description: Millburn : Behrman House, [2021] | Includes bibliographical
  references. | Selections from the Haggadah in Hebrew, romanized Hebrew,
  and English translation. | Summary: "This family-friendly traditional
  Haggadah engages all five senses and weaves in activities to promote a
  full-body connection to the Passover story and rituals"-- Provided by
  publisher.
Identifiers: LCCN 2020040588 | ISBN 9781681150611 (paperback) | ISBN
  9781681150765 (kindle edition)
Subjects: LCSH: Haggadah--Adaptations. | Seder--Liturgy--Texts. |
  Judaism--Liturgy--Texts.
Classification: LCC BM674.795 I837 2021 | DDC 296.4/5371--dc23
LC record available at https://lccn.loc.gov/2020040588

INTRODUCTION

A seder is a joyful experience. In this haggadah, we invite you to fully engage yourself—body, mind, and soul—in the miracle of redemption and freedom that is Passover.

Using this haggadah, we will connect with familiar rituals in a new way. By moving our bodies, expanding our minds, engaging our senses, and connecting with our spirits, we will *feel* the transition from slavery to freedom. We will explore traditions from around the world, from the Moroccan custom of passing a platter of matzah overhead to symbolize the "passing over," to the Bukharian reenactment of the flight from Egypt. We will consider how the familiar words and rituals of the seder resonate with the struggles of today's world.

We invite you to customize *Seder in Motion* to match participants' ages, comfort levels, and physical abilities. Challenge participants to be creative and come up with their own movements. Every year you may want to focus on different aspects of the seder, preserving what you most enjoy and experimenting with new ideas.

Your seder may include people who are physically distant, participating by phone or video link. Engage those participants by using the ideas on page 46, and look for the *CONNECTION* feature located at key points throughout the book.

Through active participation, *Seder in Motion* encourages all of us to feel a personal connection to the story of the Exodus and the flight from slavery to freedom. We hope that through this haggadah you will experience the seder's eternal message of freedom and joy, and pass on this feeling from generation to generation.

Wishing you all the joys of freedom and redemption!

Ron and Leora Isaacs

THE SEARCH FOR CHAMEITZ

*T*raditionally we remove *chameitz* (bread, pasta, and most grains) from our homes before Passover starts. The Torah says we should not eat any leavened food during Passover as a reminder of the Israelites' flight from Egypt. They left in such a hurry that the dough they had prepared for the journey did not have enough time to rise.

The ceremonial search for leavened food—called *b'dikat chameitz*—is a way to prepare ourselves physically and spiritually for the beginning of the holiday. It takes place after sundown on the night before the first Passover seder, once all other *chameitz* has been removed from the house or stored away.

The objects needed for the ceremony are:

- a candle or flashlight
- a feather
- a wooden spoon
- a paper bag for collecting the *chameitz*
- ten pieces of bread or other leavened food (each can be wrapped in a napkin)

MIND AND BODY

The Zohar, a Jewish book of mysticism, associates the search for chameitz with spiritual cleansing.

As we rid our homes of leavened food, we use the opportunity to focus on personal chameitz. We cleanse ourselves of pretense. As we search in the dark corners of our house for bread crumbs, we imagine searching the dark corners of our minds for negative inclinations.

With each brush of the feather, we envision sweeping away our bad habits. We meditate: "As I cleanse my house of chameitz, let me rid myself of _____."

Before you start, hide the ten pieces of bread around the house. (Some people note where the pieces are hidden to be sure they are all found.)

Light the candle and recite:

בָּרוּךְ אַתָּה, יְיָ אֱלֹהֵינוּ, מֶלֶךְ הָעוֹלָם, אֲשֶׁר קִדְּשָׁנוּ בְּמִצְוֹתָיו וְצִוָּנוּ עַל בִּעוּר חָמֵץ.

Baruch Atah, Adonai Eloheinu, Melech ha'olam, asher kid'shanu b'mitzvotav v'tzivanu al bi'ur chameitz.

Praised are You, Adonai our God, Ruler of the universe, who makes us holy through *mitzvot* by instructing us to remove *chameitz* [from our homes].

Holding the lit candle or flashlight, proceed around the house searching for chameitz, looking into the darkest corners. Whenever you find one of the hidden pieces, use the feather and spoon to scoop it into the paper bag.

Once you have collected all of the hidden chameitz, recite:

All types of *chameitz* in my possession that I have not seen or removed should now be nullified and considered ownerless as the dust of the earth.

Save the bag for the following morning, the morning before the seder, and take the bag of chameitz outdoors and burn it.

As it burns, recite:

All types of *chameitz* in my possession that I have seen or not seen, removed or not removed, should now be nullified and considered ownerless as the dust of the earth.

GETTING READY: OTHER RITUAL ITEMS

The seder calls for a number of ritual objects and foods that you should prepare in advance.

These are the basic items you will need for the main part of the seder:

- A haggadah for each person
- Two candles and matches
- A pillow for the seder leader to lean on
- One wine cup for each person
- Wine or grape juice (enough for four cups for each participant)
- A seder plate and its foods (see page 6)
- A cup, bowl, and hand towel for washing hands
- Three pieces of matzah, with a cover, in a matzah holder or on a plate
- Matzah (enough for all participants)
- Bowls of salt water
- Bowls of *charoset*
- *Maror* (bitter herbs, often horseradish)
- *Karpas* (parsley or other green sprigs or boiled potatoes)
- Two goblets: Elijah's cup (with wine) and Miriam's cup (with water)

These extra items can make the seder livelier:

- A pillow for each guest
- Passover games, toys, or props for young children
- An extra place setting, as a reminder of those who are unable to celebrate Passover because they are oppressed or impoverished
- A hand mirror
- One scallion for each participant
- A fragrant flower or spices

MIND AND BODY

The Jewish calendar is partly based on the cycles of the moon, and Passover always starts when the moon is full. Before lighting the candles, have everyone go to a window or step outside to gaze at the full moon.

If the sky is cloudy, imagine the moon, full and bright, behind the clouds. Consider that Passover celebrants all over the world are sharing this experience.

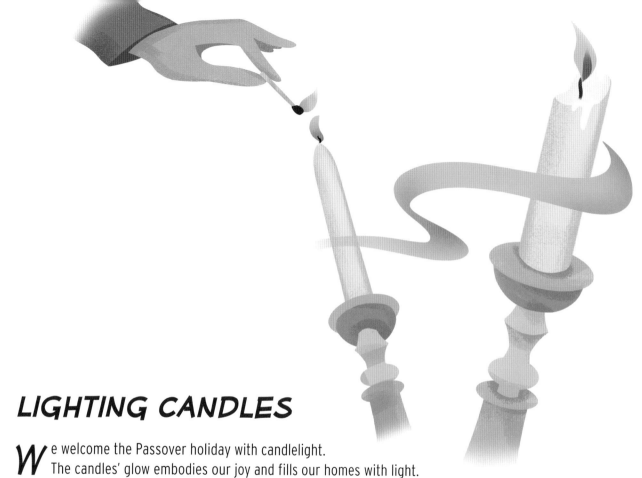

MIND AND BODY

Lift your hands over the flames and toward yourself as though drawing the light of Passover and the feeling of liberation into your mind and soul. Close your eyes and take a few deep breaths.

With each breath, exhale the worries and anxieties of the week, and inhale the joy of freedom and peace. Circle your hands above the flames three times, as if to draw in the spirit of Passover.

When you are ready, recite the traditional candle-lighting blessing. Take a moment of silence to add your personal prayers.

LIGHTING CANDLES

We welcome the Passover holiday with candlelight.
The candles' glow embodies our joy and fills our homes with light.

Light the candles. On Shabbat, add the words in parentheses:

בָּרוּךְ אַתָּה, יְיָ אֱלֹהֵינוּ, מֶלֶךְ הָעוֹלָם,
אֲשֶׁר קִדְּשָׁנוּ בְּמִצְוֹתָיו וְצִוָּנוּ
לְהַדְלִיק נֵר שֶׁל (שַׁבָּת וְשֶׁל) יוֹם טוֹב.

*Baruch Atah, Adonai Eloheinu, Melech ha'olam,
asher kid'shanu b'mitzvotav v'tzivanu
l'hadlik ner shel (Shabbat v'shel) yom tov.*

**Praised are You, Adonai our God, Ruler of the universe,
who makes us holy through *mitzvot* by instructing us to
light the (Shabbat and) festival candles.**

5

THE SEDER PLATE

A ll of the foods on the seder plate are symbols to help us remember the Exodus and the way Passover was celebrated in the time of the Temple in Jerusalem.

Charoset: A fruit and nut mixture, which symbolizes the mortar the Israelite slaves were forced to use. There are many different recipes for *charoset*. Traditional Ashkenazic *charoset* includes chopped apples, wine or grape juice, nuts, and cinnamon.

Beitzah: A roasted egg, representing the festival offering that was brought to the Temple in Jerusalem. Vegans substitute an avocado.

Z'roa: A roasted bone, often the shank bone of a lamb, symbolizing the Passover sacrifice. Vegetarians substitute a roasted beet.

Maror: A bitter herb, often horseradish, which is a reminder of the bitterness of slavery.

Karpas: A green vegetable, such as parsley or celery, evoking the rebirth of spring. Some people use boiled potatoes.

Chazeret: Some seder plates have a place for a second bitter vegetable, such as romaine lettuce, which, like *maror*, represents the bitterness of slave life.

Orange: Some people place an orange on the seder plate to symbolize how fruitful it is to include those marginalized in our society.

CONNECTION

Before beginning the seder, invite participants who are joining from afar to talk about their seder plate or one of the other items on their table— perhaps an heirloom wine goblet or a matzah cover created by one of the children—and why it is meaningful to them.

AROUND THE WORLD

Different Jewish cultures use various recipes for charoset.

For example, those from Spain and Portugal include dates, raisins, wine or grape juice, nuts, and sometimes cinnamon or other spices. Yemenite charoset adds figs, ginger, coriander, and other spices.

ORDER OF THE SEDER

*T*he Hebrew word *seder* means "order." The seder has fourteen steps, performed in a set order.

Some families sing or chant these before starting the seder itself. Do the indicated hand motion for each part of the seder as you sing or say it.

 קַדֵּשׁ **KADEISH: Say the blessing over the wine or grape juice**

Raise an imaginary cup of wine.

 וּרְחַץ **UR'CHATZ: Wash hands**

Rub the palm of one hand with the other as if washing your hands.

 כַּרְפַּס **KARPAS: Dip the vegetable in salt water and eat it**

Hold your thumb and pointer finger together and mime dipping greens in salt water.

 יַחַץ **YACHATZ: Break the middle matzah**

Hold your fists horizontally in front of you, then turn both vertically.

 מַגִּיד **MAGGID: Tell the Passover story**

Hold both palms together in front of you, then open them as if reading a book.

 רָחְצָה **ROCHTZAH: Wash hands**

Rub the palm of one hand with the other as if washing your hands.

 מוֹצִיא מַצָּה **MOTZI MATZAH: Eat matzah**

Slowly pat your hands together vertically, as if flattening dough into unleavened bread.

MAROR: Eat the bitter herb

מָרוֹר

Fan both hands in front of your face, as if cooling off from eating something bitter.

KOREICH: Eat the Hillel sandwich

כּוֹרֵךְ

Cup both hands facing each other, as if holding a sandwich.

SHULCHAN OREICH: Eat the festive meal

שֻׁלְחָן עוֹרֵךְ

Mime spooning food into your mouth.

TZAFUN: Search for and eat the *afikoman*

צָפוּן

Hold one hand palm down in front of your forehead and look around.

BAREICH: Give thanks for the meal

בָּרֵךְ

Hold the palms of both hands face up and bow your head.

HALLEL: Sing songs of praise

הַלֵּל

Extend the pointer fingers of both hands upward while raising your arms in a spiral motion.

NIRTZAH: Complete the seder

נִרְצָה

Brush your palms against each other signifying "all done."

MIND AND BODY

As you progress through the seder, chant and perform the hand motions for all the steps, starting with Kadeish, through the step you are about to do. When you reach Nirtzah at the end, recite and use hand motions for the entire order.

SAY THE BLESSING OVER WINE

Sing or say the name of this step with the hand motion.

Tonight, we will drink four cups of wine or grape juice, one for each of the four promises of freedom that the Torah tells us God made to our ancestors in Egypt.

I will free you from the labors of the Egyptians;
I will deliver you from their bondage;
I will redeem you with an outstretched arm and with great judgments;
I will take you to be my people and I will be your God.
(Exodus 6:6-7)

If you choose, stand for the Kiddush.

בָּרוּךְ אַתָּה, יְיָ אֱלֹהֵינוּ, מֶלֶךְ הָעוֹלָם,
בּוֹרֵא פְּרִי הַגָּפֶן.

Baruch Atah, Adonai Eloheinu, Melech ha'olam, borei p'ri hagafen.

Praised are You, Adonai our God, Ruler of the universe, who creates the fruit of the vine.

MIND AND BODY

Mitzrayim, the Hebrew word for Egypt, also means "narrow space." Think of one or two things that constrain you, then consider what it would be like to be freed from your own narrow space.

Breathe in and tighten the muscles of your whole body. Scrunch up your face, shoulders, arms, and legs. Now, let out your breath and relax your muscles. Can you feel the freedom?

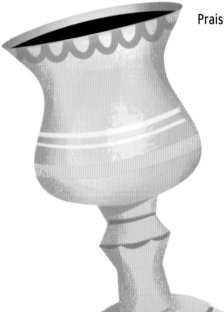

LEFT LEANING?

Leaning left while eating or drinking was the practice of nobility and free people in ancient Greek and Roman cultures. They reclined on couches, leaning on their left arm, leaving their right hand free to dip and taste.

Continue reciting the Kiddush:

בָּרוּךְ אַתָּה, יְיָ אֱלֹהֵינוּ, מֶלֶךְ הָעוֹלָם, אֲשֶׁר בָּחַר בָּנוּ
מִכָּל עָם, וְרוֹמְמָנוּ מִכָּל לָשׁוֹן וְקִדְּשָׁנוּ בְּמִצְוֹתָיו. וַתִּתֶּן לָנוּ
יְיָ אֱלֹהֵינוּ בְּאַהֲבָה (שַׁבָּתוֹת לִמְנוּחָה וּ) מוֹעֲדִים לְשִׂמְחָה,
חַגִּים וּזְמַנִּים לְשָׂשׂוֹן אֶת יוֹם (הַשַּׁבָּת הַזֶּה וְאֶת יוֹם) חַג הַמַּצּוֹת הַזֶּה,
זְמַן חֵרוּתֵנוּ (בְּאַהֲבָה) מִקְרָא קֹדֶשׁ, זֵכֶר לִיצִיאַת מִצְרָיִם.
כִּי בָנוּ בָחַרְתָּ וְאוֹתָנוּ קִדַּשְׁתָּ מִכָּל הָעַמִּים, (וְשַׁבָּת) וּמוֹעֲדֵי קָדְשֶׁךָ
(בְּאַהֲבָה וּבְרָצוֹן) בְּשִׂמְחָה וּבְשָׂשׂוֹן הִנְחַלְתָּנוּ. בָּרוּךְ אַתָּה יְיָ,
מְקַדֵּשׁ (הַשַּׁבָּת וְ) יִשְׂרָאֵל וְהַזְּמַנִּים.

*Baruch Atah, Adonai Eloheinu, Melech ha'olam, asher bachar banu
mikol am, v'rom'manu mikol lashon, v'kid'shanu b'mitzvotav. Vatiten lanu
Adonai Eloheinu b'ahavah (Shabbatot limnuchah u-) mo'adim l'simchah,
chagim uz'manim l'sason et yom (haShabbat hazeh v'et yom) chag hamatzot hazeh,
z'man cheiruteinu (b'ahavah) mikra kodesh, zeicher litzi'at Mitzrayim.
Ki vanu vacharta v'otanu kidashta mikol ha'amim, (v'Shabbat) umo'adei kodsh'cha
(b'ahavah uv'ratzon) b'simchah uv'sason hinchaltanu. Baruch Atah Adonai,
m'kadeish (haShabbat v'-) Yisrael v'haz'manim.*

Praised are You, Adonai our God, Ruler of the universe, who chose us from among the peoples and languages
by giving us the special gift of *mitzvot*. Out of love, You have given us (Shabbat for rest and) festive holidays to celebrate,
including (this Shabbat and) Passover, our time of freedom, (with love) a sacred time to help us remember the
Exodus from Egypt. You have chosen us, separating us from other peoples by (Shabbat and) special festivals
(that we happily celebrate). Praised are You, Adonai, who makes (Shabbat and) the people Israel and its festivals special.

~~~~~~~~~~

בָּרוּךְ אַתָּה, יְיָ אֱלֹהֵינוּ, מֶלֶךְ
הָעוֹלָם, שֶׁהֶחֱיָנוּ וְקִיְּמָנוּ
וְהִגִּיעָנוּ לַזְּמַן הַזֶּה.

*Baruch Atah, Adonai Eloheinu, Melech
ha'olam, shehecheyanu v'kiy'manu
v'higi'anu laz'man hazeh.*

Praised are You, Adonai our God, Ruler of the universe,
who has given us life, sustained us, and brought us to this moment.

*Be seated if you are standing.
Read together the first of the four promises:*

"I will free you from the labors of the Egyptians."
(Exodus 6:6)

Drink while leaning to the left.

MIND AND BODY

*As you sip the wine
or grape juice, take it
in with all your senses.
Hear the sound as it
flows into your glass.
Appreciate its rich
color. Inhale its aroma.
Swish it in your mouth.
Absorb its fragrance,
its flavor, and its
essence.*

WASH HANDS

Sing or say the name of the previous step, adding this one, with hand motions.

We wash our hands to prepare ourselves for the seder.

Using a pitcher or cup, pour water over each hand, either at a sink or at the table with a bowl to catch the water.

MIND AND BODY

Stretch your body like a tree to embody the rebirth of nature in spring: Standing or remaining seated, raise your arms high like the blooming branches of a tree. Press your feet into the ground like the roots. If you are able, balance on one leg and draw your other foot up to your ankle or shin, as if you are a growing tree.

MIND AND BODY

As you wash your hands, close your eyes and feel the water flowing over and between your fingers. Take a deep breath. Feel the water begin to evaporate off your hands. Imagine that you are washing away negative thoughts and feelings. In what way do your hands feel different after washing them? In what way do you feel different?

DIP THE VEGETABLE

Sing or say the names of the steps so far, with hand motions.

Spring is a time of rebirth, when plants and animals awaken after sleeping all winter.

As we dip our *karpas* in salt water, we remember the salty tears of our enslaved ancestors. At the same time we feel the hope that this new spring season brings us.

Dip the vegetable in salt water and recite:

בָּרוּךְ אַתָּה, יְיָ אֱלֹהֵינוּ, מֶלֶךְ הָעוֹלָם,
בּוֹרֵא פְּרִי הָאֲדָמָה.

Baruch Atah, Adonai Eloheinu, Melech ha'olam, borei p'ri ha'adamah.

Praised are You, Adonai our God, Ruler of the universe, who creates the fruit of the earth.

Eat the karpas.

BREAK THE MIDDLE MATZAH

Sing or say the names of the steps so far, with hand motions.

There are many explanations for why we stack three pieces of matzah. One of the most popular is that the three *matzot* represent the three groupings of Jews in Temple times: the Kohanim (priests), the Levites (assistant priests), and the Israelites (regular folks). They are all stacked together to remind us that we are one people.

Uncover the three matzot.

Hold up the middle matzah for everyone to see, and break it into two.

Put the smaller piece back in the matzah holder with the other two whole pieces.

Wrap the larger piece in a bag or napkin—this is the afikoman.

Let someone hide the afikoman; participants will search for it later.

AROUND THE WORLD

Try the Moroccan custom of breaking the middle matzah into two pieces resembling the Hebrew letter hey (ה), standing for HaShem, Hebrew for God's name.

AROUND THE WORLD

Some people add a fourth matzah to the holder and call it the "Matzah of Hope." If you choose to do this, lift it up, saying it is a symbol for all those who are not free, then set it aside on the table.

TELL THE PASSOVER STORY

Sing or say the names of the steps so far, with hand motions.

MAH NISHTANAH: THE FOUR QUESTIONS

*T*he rabbis knew that we must actively engage everyone in the seder. We therefore start the Passover story with four questions, asked by participants and designed to make us all pay attention to what we are doing tonight.

Some families follow the custom of having the youngest child recite or sing the Four Questions. Others sing the Four Questions together or assign different parts to individual seder participants.

THE FOURTH QUESTION

Before the eleventh century, the fourth question was not about reclining but rather: "On all other nights we eat roasted or boiled meat; on this night we eat only roasted meat." This question was replaced when people's daily diets became more varied.

MIND AND BODY

Challenge participants to come up with motions to accompany the Four Questions. For example, for Mah Nishtanah, you could hold your palms up shoulder-high in a questioning gesture. For haleilot (nights), you could tilt your head and rest it on your hands as if sleeping.

14

MIND AND BODY

"When do we eat?" may seem like the most important question at a Passover seder.

Take a deep breath before each of the Four Questions. Breathe out the word patience.

Mah Nishtanah reminds us of the value of patience, taking time to listen to the concerns of others and thoughtfully address their questions.

מַה נִּשְׁתַּנָּה הַלַּיְלָה הַזֶּה מִכָּל הַלֵּילוֹת?   *Mah nishtanah halailah hazeh mikol haleilot?*

How is this night different from all other nights?

שֶׁבְּכָל הַלֵּילוֹת אָנוּ אוֹכְלִין חָמֵץ וּמַצָּה;   *Sheb'chol haleilot anu och'lin chameitz umatzah;*
הַלַּיְלָה הַזֶּה כֻּלּוֹ מַצָּה.   *halailah hazeh kulo matzah.*

On all other nights we eat leavened bread or matzah.
On this night, why do we eat only matzah?

שֶׁבְּכָל הַלֵּילוֹת אָנוּ אוֹכְלִין שְׁאָר יְרָקוֹת;   *Sheb'chol haleilot anu och'lin sh'ar y'rakot;*
הַלַּיְלָה הַזֶּה מָרוֹר.   *halailah hazeh maror.*

On all other nights we eat all kinds of vegetables.
On this night, why do we eat bitter herbs?

שֶׁבְּכָל הַלֵּילוֹת אֵין אָנוּ מַטְבִּילִין אֲפִילוּ פַּעַם   *Sheb'chol haleilot ein anu matbilin afilu pa'am*
אֶחָת; הַלַּיְלָה הַזֶּה שְׁתֵּי פְעָמִים.   *achat; halailah hazeh sh'tei f'amim.*

On all other nights we don't dip our vegetables even once.
On this night, why do we dip twice?

שֶׁבְּכָל הַלֵּילוֹת אָנוּ אוֹכְלִין בֵּין יוֹשְׁבִין וּבֵין   *Sheb'chol haleilot anu och'lin bein yoshvin uvein*
מְסֻבִּין; הַלַּיְלָה הַזֶּה כֻּלָּנוּ מְסֻבִּין.   *m'subin; halailah hazeh kulanu m'subin.*

On all other nights we eat sitting up straight or reclining.
On this night, why do we recline?

WHO TOOK MY MATZAH?

Maimonides, the great medieval philosopher, instructed parents to engage in unusual behavior at the seder, such as snatching matzah or removing the seder plate from the table, in order to cause the children to ask questions. What unusual behavior could you engage in to elicit new questions from your participants?

THE FOUR CHILDREN:
FOUR KINDS OF LEARNERS

E ach of us learns differently. The rabbis described four children, each with a different learning style. These children remind us to recognize and honor our differences in everything we do, including how we celebrate the seder.

Some children will ask with curiosity, "What is the meaning of the rules and laws that God commanded us?" We can reply by describing all of the customs and laws of Passover, with as much detail and explanation as the child desires.

Some children will defiantly challenge, "Why do you celebrate Passover?" They aren't even sure they want to be part of the celebration. We can explain that we celebrate because God took our people out of slavery. We can also point out that if they include themselves, instead of setting themselves apart, they will share in our joy of freedom.

Some children will innocently ask, "What happened? Can you tell me the story?" They know this is a celebration, but they don't know why. We can respond gently that God freed us from slavery and took us out of Egypt.

And some children will not recognize that anything unusual is happening. We can use creative ways to help them understand the relevance of the Passover story to their lives. When we do this, we help them understand what God did for us when our ancestors were freed from slavery in Egypt.

B'CHOL DOR VADOR: IN EVERY GENERATION

At the heart of the haggadah is the *maggid*, the story of how we became a free people. In fact, the words *haggadah* and *maggid* come from the same Hebrew root, which means "to tell a story." The Torah commands us to tell and retell this story in every generation, and the Talmud adds a personal connection.

בְּכָל דּוֹר וָדוֹר חַיָּב אָדָם לִרְאוֹת אֶת עַצְמוֹ
כְּאִלּוּ הוּא יָצָא מִמִּצְרַיִם.

B'chol dor vador chayav adam lir'ot et atzmo k'ilu hu yatza miMitzrayim.

In every generation, even today when we are blessed to live in freedom, each of us should feel as though we personally were freed from Egypt.

JOIN US

If you have left an extra place setting, look at it now and say, "Let all who are hungry come and join us." This empty seat is a tangible symbol of those in need. Consider what you could do to ensure that more people are able to celebrate their freedom in the coming year.

UNBOUND

Two blessings in the traditional daily morning service celebrate being released from bondage.

Praised are You, Adonai our God, Ruler of the universe, who releases those who are bound.

Praised are You, Adonai our God, Ruler of the universe, who has made me free.

We begin telling the story of the Exodus with an invitation for all who are hungry to come and eat, to experience the seder, and to taste freedom.

MIND AND BODY

Take turns passing a hand mirror around the table. Visualize yourself as a slave in ancient Egypt. If you want, share what you see.

Now contrast that with a feeling of freedom. Either rise or remain seated; stretch your arms toward the ceiling and spread them outward (being careful not to hit your neighbor). Gently arch your back and gaze upward. Loosen your muscles by doing shoulder rolls.

Feel your connection to the ancient Israelites and all people who have been—and are— enslaved. Acknowledge the many ways in which people can be enslaved—by inequality, by bigotry and hatred, by small-mindedness. Can we find the courage in our hearts to free ourselves and others?

Uncover the plate of matzah, raise it high, and recite:

הָא לַחְמָא עַנְיָא דִי אֲכָלוּ אַבְהָתָנָא
בְּאַרְעָא דְמִצְרָיִם.

Ha lachma anya di achalu avhatana b'ar'a d'Mitzrayim.

This is the bread of poverty that our ancestors ate in the land of Egypt.

Let all who are hungry come and join us for the meal.
Now we are here.
Next year may we be in the land of Israel.
Now we are still slaves.
Next year may we be truly free.

Fill the second cup of wine or grape juice but do not drink.

OUR STORY BEGINS

O ur story begins some thirty-five hundred years ago. The Israelites had lived peacefully in Egypt for many years. Then a new Pharaoh arose. He feared the Israelites. He feared they were growing too quickly, in numbers and in strength. And so he enslaved them, hoping to break their spirits so that he would no longer have to be afraid.

Every year, we retell the miraculous story of how God liberated our ancestors from slavery in Egypt. When we hear this story, we rededicate ourselves to liberating all who are enslaved today, throughout the world.

עֲבָדִים הָיִינוּ, עַתָּה בְּנֵי-חוֹרִין.   *Avadim hayinu, atah b'nei-chorin.*

We were slaves to Pharaoh in Egypt, but God brought us out
with a mighty hand and an outstretched arm.
Had God not brought us out of Egypt, we would still be slaves to Pharaoh
—and so would our children and our grandchildren.

AROUND THE WORLD

Sephardic Jews pretend to beat each other with scallions to symbolize what it felt like to be whipped by the Egyptian taskmasters. If you choose, prepare enough scallions for each seder participant. Beat each other gently with the scallions while singing Avadim Hayinu.

THE BIRTH OF MOSES

Even in slavery, it is said that the Israelites kept their faith and held fast to their traditions. They continued to raise families. Their numbers increased. Pharaoh became more afraid and even more determined to destroy them. He ordered all Israelite boys drowned in the Nile River.

One Israelite mother, Yocheved, risked her life to save her newborn son. She hid him in a small straw basket in the reeds along the waterfront of the Nile River. The boy's sister, Miriam, watched over him.

Pharaoh's daughter, who was bathing in the river, found the basket. Her heart filled with compassion. She named the baby Moses, which means "drawn from the water," and later made him her son.

Miriam convinced Pharaoh's daughter to let Yocheved be Moses's nursemaid.

MOSES FLEES TO MIDIAN

Moses knew he was an Israelite, even though he was raised as Pharaoh's grandson.

One day, Moses saw an Egyptian taskmaster whipping an Israelite slave. Moses could not simply stand by. He stepped in and saved the slave, but he killed the taskmaster.

Afraid for his own life, Moses fled to the desert of Midian. There, he met a Midianite priest named Jethro. Moses married Jethro's daughter Zipporah.

One day, while tending Jethro's sheep, Moses came upon a fiery bush. To his amazement, the bush burned without being consumed. God spoke to Moses from the bush, saying: "I am the God of your ancestors. I have seen the suffering of My people. Go to Pharaoh and bring My people out of Egypt."

THE PLAGUES

Moses returned to Egypt. With his brother, Aaron, he demanded that Pharaoh free the Israelites. Pharaoh refused. God brought ten terrible plagues upon Egypt to convince Pharaoh to free the Israelites.

Recite the plagues aloud, removing a drop of wine or grape juice from your cup with your pinkie finger or a spoon as you recite each one.

In this way we remember that the plagues caused the ancient Egyptians to suffer, and so our joy is lessened.

MIND AND BODY

Think about this: What troubles you or the world today? What do you see and hear? What can you do to help eliminate these plagues?

How does it feel to think about these questions? Where in your body do you feel it?

AROUND THE WORLD

Follow the Moroccan custom of passing a platter of matzahs over the head of each seder participant to symbolize how the angel of God passed over the homes of the Israelites on the night of the tenth plague.

דָּם	DAM	BLOOD
צְפַרְדֵּעַ	TZ'FARDEI'A	FROGS
כִּנִּים	KINIM	LICE
עָרוֹב	AROV	WILD BEASTS
דֶּבֶר	DEVER	CATTLE DISEASE
שְׁחִין	SH'CHIN	BOILS
בָּרָד	BARAD	HAIL
אַרְבֶּה	ARBEH	LOCUSTS
חֹשֶׁךְ	CHOSHECH	DARKNESS
מַכַּת בְּכוֹרוֹת	MAKAT B'CHOROT	DEATH OF THE FIRSTBORN

CONNECTION

Have participants take turns on-screen making up hand motions for the plagues. For example, to show the water of the Nile turning to blood, make a ripple motion in front of you with one finger. And to show frogs, hop your fingers across the table.

Through nine plagues, Pharaoh remained defiant, refusing to let the Israelites go.

But the tenth plague was the most terrible.

The angel of God slew the Egyptians' firstborn sons but passed over the Israelites' homes.

A great cry arose throughout all of Egypt.

Pharaoh's will was finally broken. He agreed to let the Israelites go.

MIND AND BODY

With the Sea of Reeds in front of them and the Egyptians behind them, the Israelites surely felt trapped. Is there something that keeps you from moving forward in your life? Picture the obstacle you face. Imagine yourself overcoming that obstacle, just as the Israelites passed through the Sea of Reeds. Experience the jubilation of achieving your goal. How does this make you feel? How can you describe this feeling in your body?

THE GREAT ESCAPE

The Israelites packed up and left in a hurry. There wasn't even enough time for their bread to rise.

But it wasn't long before Pharaoh's heart hardened again. He raced with his army and chariots to recapture the fleeing Israelites.

The Israelites heard the horses, chariots, and soldiers behind them, just as they saw the Sea of Reeds blocking their path.

They were trapped.

"Why did you bring us out of Egypt just to die here?" they cried out to Moses.

At what seemed like the last moment,
God told Moses to raise his staff.
Miraculously, the waters parted.
The Israelites hurried through.

When all the Israelites had crossed to safety, the waters closed over the pursuing Egyptians. Moses and his sister Miriam led the people in joyous song. The women danced with their timbrels and sang songs of praise.

AROUND THE WORLD

Reenact the flight from Egypt with a Bukharian custom. Wrap a piece of matzah in your napkin, making a knapsack. Throw your knapsack over your shoulder and hunch over. Form a procession with seder participants and march around the seder table singing "Go Down Moses" or another song, as if you are leaving Egypt.

DAYEINU: IT WOULD HAVE BEEN ENOUGH

The song "Dayeinu" expresses thanks for everything God did for us during the flight from Egypt. It recalls every step on our path to redemption: the Exodus from Egypt, the splitting of the sea, the sustenance in the wilderness, and the arrival in the land of Israel. For each action we say *dayeinu*: "that alone would have been enough, and for that alone we are grateful."

Sing the song together and/or read the English translation.

אִלּוּ הוֹצִיאָנוּ מִמִּצְרַיִם–דַּיֵּנוּ! *Ilu hotzi'anu miMitzrayim–dayeinu!*

אִלּוּ עָשָׂה בָהֶם שְׁפָטִים–דַּיֵּנוּ! *Ilu asah vahem sh'fatim–dayeinu!*

אִלּוּ עָשָׂה בֵאלֹהֵיהֶם–דַּיֵּנוּ! *Ilu asah veloheihem–dayeinu!*

Had God only...

Taken us out of Egypt–*dayeinu!*
Judged the Egyptians–*dayeinu!*
Destroyed the Egyptians' idols–*dayeinu!*
Slain the Egyptians' firstborns–*dayeinu!*
Given us the Egyptians' wealth–*dayeinu!*
Divided the sea for us–*dayeinu!*
Led us through dry land–*dayeinu!*
Drowned our oppressors–*dayeinu!*
Cared for us in the desert for forty years–*dayeinu!*
Given us manna–*dayeinu!*
Given us the Shabbat–*dayeinu!*
Brought us to Mount Sinai–*dayeinu!*
Given us the Torah–*dayeinu!*
Brought us into the land of Israel–*dayeinu!*

MIND AND BODY

Each verse of "Dayeinu" represents one step toward freedom. Act out the march toward freedom by stomping your feet to the tempo of the song and clapping your hands or banging softly on the table. Shout the word dayeinu at the end of each verse.

GOD'S PROMISE

The redemption from Egypt was only the beginning of our people's journey from slavery to freedom, from sadness to joy, from being strangers in Egypt to being a great and free nation. It was the fulfillment of God's promise to Abraham and Sarah that their children would be a great people.

Recite or sing while raising your cup of wine.

וְהִיא שֶׁעָמְדָה לַאֲבוֹתֵינוּ וְלָנוּ. *V'hi she'amdah la'avoteinu v'lanu.*

In every generation enemies have risen up against us, and God has saved us from their hands.

27

PESACH, MATZAH, MAROR

R abbi Gamliel believed that the three most important symbols at the seder are the *pesach* offering (symbolized by the shank bone), the matzah, and the *maror* (bitter herb). These three items embody the bitterness of slavery and the flight to freedom.

Point to or hold up the shank bone or roasted beet on the seder plate.

This roasted bone (beet), the *pesach*, represents the Paschal lamb, the offering that our ancestors brought to the Temple in Jerusalem to celebrate Passover. It reminds us of how the Israelites marked their doors with lambs' blood on the night of the tenth plague. The Torah uses the word *pesach* (Passover) to describe how the angel of God passed over the Israelites and only harmed the firstborn Egyptians.

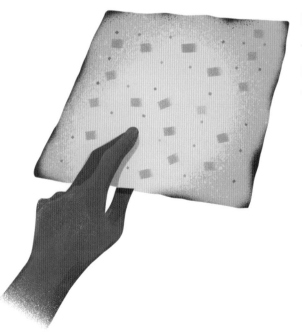

Point to or hold up the matzah.

This unleavened bread, matzah, reminds us of how the Israelites left Egypt in such a hurry that they did not have time for their dough to rise and become bread.

Point to or hold up the maror (bitter herb) on the seder plate.

This bitter herb, *maror*, reminds us of how the Egyptians made the lives of the Israelites bitter with hard and punishing work.

FREE AT LAST

When the Israelites safely crossed the Sea of Reeds, they sang songs of praise to God. Filled with gratitude, we, too, give thanks. We sing praises to God for performing miracles for our ancestors and for us.

בְּצֵאת יִשְׂרָאֵל מִמִּצְרָיִם,   *B'tzeit Yisrael miMitzrayim,*

בֵּית יַעֲקֹב מֵעַם לֹעֵז.   *beit Ya'akov, mei'am lo'eiz.*

הָיְתָה יְהוּדָה לְקָדְשׁוֹ,   *Haitah Yehudah l'kodsho,*

יִשְׂרָאֵל מַמְשְׁלוֹתָיו.   *Yisrael mamsh'lotav.*

הַיָּם רָאָה וַיָּנֹס,   *Hayam ra'ah vayanos,*

הַיַּרְדֵּן יִסֹּב לְאָחוֹר.   *haYardein yisov l'achor.*

הֶהָרִים רָקְדוּ כְאֵילִים,   *Heharim rak'du ch'eilim*

גְּבָעוֹת כִּבְנֵי צֹאן.   *G'va'ot kiv'nei tzon.*

When Israel came forth from Egypt,
The house of Jacob from a people of strange language,
Judah became God's sanctuary,
Israel, God's dominion.
The sea saw it and fled,
The Jordan turned backward.
Mountains skipped like lambs,
Hills like young sheep.
(Psalm 114)

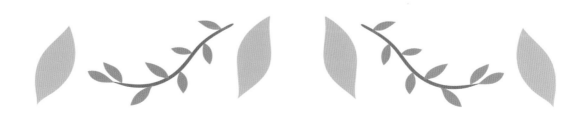

29

THE SECOND CUP OF WINE

Raise the second cup of wine or grape juice and read together the second of the four promises:

*I*t is our duty to give thanks, sing praises, and offer blessings to God who did these miracles for our ancestors and for us.

"I will deliver you." (Exodus 6:6)

בָּרוּךְ אַתָּה, יְיָ אֱלֹהֵינוּ, מֶלֶךְ הָעוֹלָם, בּוֹרֵא פְּרִי הַגָּפֶן.

Baruch Atah, Adonai Eloheinu, Melech ha'olam, borei p'ri hagafen.

Praised are You, Adonai our God, Ruler of the universe, who creates the fruit of the vine.

Drink from the second cup of wine or grape juice while leaning to the left.

MIND AND BODY

Water is a symbol of life because it nourishes all living things. Pour the water over your hands before reciting the blessing. Notice the sensation of the water trickling over your hands. Flutter or flick your fingers and watch the droplets shimmer. With your palms open, feel the water begin to evaporate. Reflect on this sensation. How does wet skin feel different from dry skin?

WASH HANDS

Sing or say the names of the steps so far, with hand motions.

*T*he seder is no ordinary meal. It is filled with ritual, questioning, telling, singing, and of course, eating.

In Jewish tradition, eating is a holy act. The ancient rabbis compared the dinner table to the altar in the Temple. As we wash our hands, as the priests did, we elevate the ordinary act of eating into one that is extraordinary and sacred.

רׇחְצָה • ROCHTZAH

30

Using a pitcher or cup, pour water over each hand, either at the sink or at the table with a bowl to catch the water, and then recite the blessing:

בָּרוּךְ אַתָּה, יְיָ אֱלֹהֵינוּ, מֶלֶךְ הָעוֹלָם,
אֲשֶׁר קִדְּשָׁנוּ בְּמִצְוֹתָיו וְצִוָּנוּ עַל נְטִילַת יָדָיִם.

Baruch Atah, Adonai Eloheinu, Melech ha'olam, asher kid'shanu b'mitzvotav v'tzivanu al n'tilat yadayim.

Praised are You, Adonai our God, Ruler of the universe,
who makes us holy through *mitzvot* by instructing us to wash our hands.

EAT MATZAH

Sing or say the names of the steps so far, with hand motions.

Before we eat the matzah, we say two blessings of thanks. The first expresses appreciation for all kinds of bread, including matzah. The second is a blessing just for the matzah.

Pass out pieces of the upper and middle matzot for eating.
The last piece is saved for later, to be used for the Hillel sandwich.

Lift the three pieces of matzah (really two and a half pieces) and say the following two blessings.

בָּרוּךְ אַתָּה, יְיָ אֱלֹהֵינוּ, מֶלֶךְ
הָעוֹלָם, הַמּוֹצִיא לֶחֶם מִן הָאָרֶץ.

Baruch Atah, Adonai Eloheinu, Melech ha'olam, hamotzi lechem min ha'aretz.

Praised are You, Adonai our God, Ruler of the universe, who brings forth bread from the earth.

בָּרוּךְ אַתָּה, יְיָ אֱלֹהֵינוּ, מֶלֶךְ הָעוֹלָם,
אֲשֶׁר קִדְּשָׁנוּ בְּמִצְוֹתָיו וְצִוָּנוּ עַל
אֲכִילַת מַצָּה.

Baruch Atah, Adonai Eloheinu, Melech ha'olam, asher kid'shanu b'mitzvotav v'tzivanu al achilat matzah.

Praised are You, Adonai our God, Ruler of the universe, who makes us holy through
mitzvot by instructing us to eat matzah.

EAT THE BITTER HERB

Sing or say the names of the steps so far, with hand motions.

The bitter *maror* reminds us of the pain our ancestors felt as slaves in Egypt. The *charoset* we dip it into reminds us of the mortar they used for cementing the bricks when they built Pharaoh's storehouses.

Say the blessing and eat the maror dipped in charoset.

בָּרוּךְ אַתָּה, יְיָ אֱלֹהֵינוּ, מֶלֶךְ הָעוֹלָם,
אֲשֶׁר קִדְּשָׁנוּ בְּמִצְוֹתָיו וְצִוָּנוּ עַל
אֲכִילַת מָרוֹר.

Baruch Atah, Adonai Eloheinu, Melech ha'olam, asher kid'shanu b'mitzvotav v'tzivanu al achilat maror.

Praised are You, Adonai our God, Ruler of the universe, who makes us holy through *mitzvot* by instructing us to eat *maror*.

MIND AND BODY

Pay attention to the sensations you feel as you bite into the maror. Do your eyes water? Do your lips purse? Does your chest tighten?

Think about how you feel when you are embittered. Now focus on the sweetness of the charoset. How does it affect the way you experience the maror? How might you temper times of bitterness with the sweetness of hope or gratitude?

Can you notice both the taste of the bitter and the taste of the sweet at once? Can you balance the emotions of bitterness and of gratitude?

32

EAT THE HILLEL SANDWICH

Sing or say the names of the steps so far, with hand motions.

*I*n Temple times, Rabbi Hillel made a sandwich with matzah, meat from the Passover offering, and *maror*. Why? So he could eat all of the ingredients of the bitterness of slavery together, and in one bite fulfill the biblical verse, "with *matzot* and bitter herbs they shall eat it [the Passover offering]" (Exodus 12:8).

Today, we follow Rabbi Hillel's example and make our own Hillel sandwich. Since we no longer bring sacrifices, our ingredients include matzah, *maror*, and *charoset*.

Distribute pieces of the bottom matzah (the only one left of the original three). Make a sandwich with charoset and maror inside.

HOW DO YOU LIKE YOUR EGGS?

Many families serve hard-boiled eggs at the beginning of the meal because they are a symbol of spring, renewal, and the new life the Israelites enjoyed after being liberated from Egypt. Some say that we use hard-boiled eggs because the more you boil an egg, the harder it gets, just as the Israelites became stronger (more numerous) the more that Pharaoh punished them.

EAT THE FESTIVE MEAL

Sing or say the names of the steps so far, with hand motions.

Enjoy the meal!

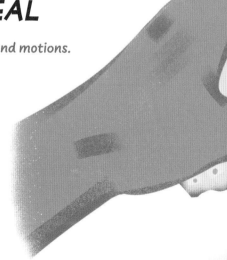

MIND AND BODY

Play a fast-moving game. Go around the table and give each participant five seconds to name the most interesting thing they have ever found (real or metaphorical). Keep going until they run out of ideas.

MIND AND BODY

Close your eyes. Inhale deeply. Exhale deeply. Focus on how your body feels after the seder feast. How does it feel to be pleasantly full? Think about all that went into providing you with this meal and express gratitude for:

- the seeds that were cultivated over hundreds of years to produce the crops

- the nutrient-rich soil that your food grew in

- the clean water supply that provided hydration to the roots in the soil

- the weather that provided good growing conditions

- the farmers who planned, planted, tended, and harvested the crops

What can you add to this list?

צָפוּן • **TZAFUN**

SEARCH FOR AND EAT THE AFIKOMAN

Sing or say the names of the steps so far, with hand motions.

It is traditional for everyone to eat a small piece of the *afikoman* at the conclusion of the meal. That way, matzah is the last food you taste at the seder. But first the *afikoman* must be found!

When the afikoman is found, distribute a piece of the matzah to each participant to eat. A small reward or prize may be offered to the person who finds the afikoman or to all those who searched for it.

34

GIVE THANKS FOR THE MEAL

Sing or say the names of the steps so far, with hand motions.

After the meal, we thank God for all the gifts we have received. These include the gifts of having friends, family, and ample food to eat.

Fill the third cup of wine or grape juice but do not drink.

בָּרוּךְ אַתָּה, יְיָ אֱלֹהֵינוּ, מֶלֶךְ הָעוֹלָם, הַזָּן אֶת הָעוֹלָם כֻּלּוֹ בְּטוּבוֹ בְּחֵן בְּחֶסֶד וּבְרַחֲמִים. הוּא נוֹתֵן לֶחֶם לְכָל בָּשָׂר כִּי לְעוֹלָם חַסְדּוֹ. וּבְטוּבוֹ הַגָּדוֹל תָּמִיד לֹא חָסַר לָנוּ, וְאַל יֶחְסַר לָנוּ מָזוֹן לְעוֹלָם וָעֶד בַּעֲבוּר שְׁמוֹ הַגָּדוֹל, כִּי הוּא אֵל זָן וּמְפַרְנֵס לַכֹּל וּמֵיטִיב לַכֹּל, וּמֵכִין מָזוֹן לְכָל בְּרִיּוֹתָיו אֲשֶׁר בָּרָא. בָּרוּךְ אַתָּה, יְיָ, הַזָּן אֶת הַכֹּל.

Baruch Atah, Adonai Eloheinu, Melech ha'olam, hazan et ha'olam kulo b'tuvo b'chein b'chesed uv'rachamim. Hu notein lechem l'chol basar ki l'olam chasdo. Uv'tuvo hagadol tamid lo chasar lanu, v'al yechsar lanu mazon l'olam va'ed ba'avur sh'mo hagadol, ki hu El zan um'farneis lakol u'meitiv lakol, umeichin mazon l'chol b'riyotav asher bara. Baruch Atah, Adonai, hazan et hakol.

Praised are You, Adonai our God, Ruler of the universe, who nourishes the whole world with goodness and grace, kindness and mercy. You provide for all. Your goodness has caused us never to want for food. You prepare food for all creatures and bring sustenance to all. Praised are You, Adonai, Provider for all.

THE THIRD CUP OF WINE

Raise the third cup of wine or grape juice and read together the third of the four promises:

"I will redeem you with an outstretched arm and with great judgments." (Exodus 6:6)

בָּרוּךְ אַתָּה, יְיָ אֱלֹהֵינוּ, מֶלֶךְ הָעוֹלָם, בּוֹרֵא פְּרִי הַגָּפֶן.

Baruch Atah, Adonai Eloheinu, Melech ha'olam, borei p'ri hagafen.

Praised are You, Adonai our God, Ruler of the universe, who creates the fruit of the vine.

Drink from the third cup of wine or grape juice while leaning to the left.

MIND AND BODY

Don't just open the door for Elijah—invite seder participants to take a short walk outside. Aside from much needed exercise after the meal, a walk makes the point that instead of waiting for the Messianic age to come, you have to go out and work to bring it about.

WELCOME ELIJAH THE PROPHET

According to tradition, Elijah the prophet will one day announce the arrival of the Messiah and a time of peace and freedom for all. We therefore set out a special cup of wine and sing to welcome him.

Have someone open the door of your home to symbolically welcome Elijah.
Sing together:

אֵלִיָּהוּ הַנָּבִיא, אֵלִיָּהוּ הַתִּשְׁבִּי,
אֵלִיָּהוּ, אֵלִיָּהוּ, אֵלִיָּהוּ הַגִּלְעָדִי.
בִּמְהֵרָה בְיָמֵינוּ יָבֹא אֵלֵינוּ
עִם מָשִׁיחַ בֶּן דָּוִד.

Eliyahu hanavi, Eliyahu haTishbi,
Eliyahu, Eliyahu, Eliyahu haGiladi.
Bimheirah v'yameinu yavo eileinu
im Mashi'ach ben David.

Elijah the prophet, Elijah the Tishbite,
Elijah, Elijah, Elijah from Gilead.
Quickly in our days may he come to us
with the Messiah, son of David.

CONNECTION

Open the front door at each home. Invite participants to show their open doors on-screen.

36

TO SIP OR NOT TO SIP?

In some families the leader drinks a sip from Miriam's cup. Others pour water from the cup into individual participants' glasses. And others don't drink the water at all.

HONOR MIRIAM THE PROPHET

Our tradition teaches that Miriam's well was a miraculous source of water that accompanied the Israelites throughout their desert trek. Miriam's cup is filled with water to remind us of this well.

LIVING WATERS

The ritual of Miriam's cup was created by Stephanie Loo Ritari for a women's Rosh Chodesh group in Boston in the 1980s. She filled a cup with what she called mayim chayim (living waters) and led an accompanying guided meditation.

Fill the cup with water and recite together:

This is Miriam's cup, the cup of living water.

We remember the women of the Exodus story: Shiphrah and Puah, the midwives who refused Pharaoh's order to kill newborn Israelite boys; Yocheved, the mother of Moses; her daughter, Miriam the prophet; Batya, the daughter of Pharaoh and savior of Moses; and Zipporah, Moses's wife.

According to tradition, it was in the merit of the brave and resourceful women of that generation that the Israelites were redeemed from Egypt.

SING SONGS OF PRAISE

Sing or say the names of the steps so far, with hand motions.

The seder continues with psalms of praise to express gratitude.

Fill the fourth cup of wine or grape juice but do not drink.

הַלְלוּ אֶת יְיָ כָּל גּוֹיִם,   *Hallelu et Adonai kol goyim,*
שַׁבְּחוּהוּ כָּל הָאֻמִּים.   *shab'chuhu kol ha'umim.*
כִּי גָבַר עָלֵינוּ חַסְדּוֹ   *Ki gavar aleinu chasdo*
וֶאֱמֶת יְיָ לְעוֹלָם. הַלְלוּיָהּ.   *Ve'emet Adonai l'olam. Halleluyah.*

Praise God, all nations,
Praise God, all peoples.
God's love overwhelms us,
And God's truth endures forever. Halleluyah!

(Psalm 117)

〜〜〜〜〜〜〜

הוֹדוּ לַיְיָ כִּי טוֹב, כִּי לְעוֹלָם חַסְדּוֹ.   *Hodu LAdonai ki tov, ki l'olam chasdo.*
יֹאמַר נָא יִשְׂרָאֵל, כִּי לְעוֹלָם חַסְדּוֹ.   *Yomar na Yisrael, ki l'olam chasdo.*
יֹאמְרוּ נָא בֵית אַהֲרֹן, כִּי לְעוֹלָם חַסְדּוֹ.   *Yom'ru na veit Aharon, ki l'olam chasdo.*
יֹאמְרוּ נָא יִרְאֵי יְיָ, כִּי לְעוֹלָם חַסְדּוֹ.   *Yomru na yirei Adonai, ki l'olam chasdo.*

Give thanks to God, for God is good; God's kindness is forever.
Israel should say: God's kindness is forever.
The house of Aaron should say: God's kindness is forever.
Everyone who reveres God should say: God's kindness is forever.

(Psalm 118)

MIND AND BODY

Close your eyes and focus on one single thing for which you are grateful at this moment. Allow it to fully enter into your consciousness. As you imagine the source of your gratitude, notice what feelings you are experiencing.

Notice especially the sensations you detect in your body, especially in the area of your heart. Let appreciation and gratitude rise and fill your body and mind.

THE FOURTH CUP OF WINE

Raise the fourth cup of wine or grape juice and read together the fourth of the four promises:

"I will take you to be my people and I will be your God." (Exodus 6:7)

בָּרוּךְ אַתָּה, יְיָ אֱלֹהֵינוּ, מֶלֶךְ הָעוֹלָם,   *Baruch Atah, Adonai Eloheinu, Melech ha'olam,*
בּוֹרֵא פְּרִי הַגָּפֶן.   *borei p'ri hagafen.*

**Praised are You, Adonai our God, Ruler of the universe,
who creates the fruit of the vine.**

Drink from the fourth cup of wine or grape juice while leaning to the left.

COMPLETE THE SEDER

Sing and sign all the steps of the seder.

We have reached the end of our seder. We have used our hearts, our minds, and all of our senses to relive the miracle of being released from slavery and to rejoice in our freedom. Mindful of our many gifts, we have expressed gratitude for the bounties of nature and the wondrous rebirth of spring. We hope that the coming year will bring freedom, peace, and healing to Israel and to all who dwell on earth.

לְשָׁנָה הַבָּאָה בִּירוּשָׁלָיִם. *L'shanah haba'ah biY'rushalayim*

NEXT YEAR IN JERUSALEM!

MIND AND BODY

Pass a fragrant flower or spices around the table. Take turns inhaling deeply, and as you exhale say "l'shanah haba'ah" and express (or think to yourself) a wish for the coming year. If this wish came true, how would you express your joy physically?

AROUND THE WORLD

Some families drink a fifth cup of wine in gratitude for the State of Israel. The fifth cup represents the fifth expression of redemption in Exodus, "And I will bring you to the land..." (Exodus 6:8). Many sing Israel's national anthem, "Hatikvah."

40

AROUND THE WORLD

Some families have the practice of buying and setting aside one grain-based, non-perishable food item on each day of the omer, and donating it to a food bank on the day before Shavuot.

Consider adopting that tradition. For the first seven days of the omer, which fall during Passover, you could set aside a matzah product (such as matzah crackers, cookies, or Passover cake mix) or any non-perishable food item.

COUNT THE OMER

On the second night of Passover, we begin counting the forty-nine days (the *omer*) from the Exodus to receiving the Torah at Mount Sinai, which we celebrate on the festival of Shavuot. The countdown reflects the connection between the two holidays. The Israelites were not truly free from slavery until they received the Torah.

Rise, recite the blessing, and count the omer.

בָּרוּךְ אַתָּה, יְיָ אֱלֹהֵינוּ, מֶלֶךְ הָעוֹלָם, אֲשֶׁר קִדְּשָׁנוּ בְּמִצְוֹתָיו וְצִוָּנוּ עַל סְפִירַת הָעֹמֶר.

Baruch Atah, Adonai Eloheinu, Melech ha'olam, asher kid'shanu b'mitzvotav v'tzivanu al s'firat ha'omer.

Praised are You, Adonai our God, Ruler of the universe,
who makes us holy through *mitzvot* by instructing us to count the *omer*.

Today is the first day of the *omer*.

BARLEY TO THE TEMPLE

The omer, a measure of barley from the new harvest, was a communal offering presented at the Temple in Jerusalem on the day—the sixteenth of Nisan—on which the count toward Shavuot began.

SEDER SONGS

Sing these seder songs together.

"ECHAD MI YODEI'A": WHO KNOWS ONE?

Echad mi yodei'a? *Echad ani yodei'a: Echad Eloheinu shebashamayim uva'aretz.*

Sh'nayim mi yodei'a? *Sh'nayim ani yodei'a: Sh'nei luchot habrit, echad Eloheinu shebashamayim uva'aretz.*

Sh'loshah mi yodei'a? *Sh'loshah ani yodei'a: Sh'loshah avot, sh'nei luchot habrit, echad Eloheinu shebashamayim uva'aretz.*

Arba mi yodei'a? *Arba ani yodei'a: Arba imahot, sh'loshah avot, sh'nei luchot habrit, echad Eloheinu shebashamayim uva'aretz*

Chamishah mi yodei'a? *Chamishah ani yodei'a: Chamishah chumshei Torah, arba imahot, sh'loshah avot, sh'nei luchot habrit, echad Eloheinu shebashamayim uva'aretz.*

Shishah mi yodei'a? *Shishah ani yodei'a: Shishah sidrei Mishnah, chamishah chumshei Torah, arba imahot, sh'loshah avot, sh'nei luchot habrit, echad Eloheinu shebashamayim uva'aretz.*

Shivah mi yodei'a? *Shivah ani yodei'a: Shivah y'mei shabta, shishah sidrei Mishnah, chamishah chumshei Torah, arba imahot, sh'loshah avot, sh'nei luchot habrit, echad Eloheinu shebashamayim uva'aretz.*

Sh'monah mi yodei'a? *Sh'monah ani yodei'a: Sh'monah y'mei milah, shivah y'mei shabta, shishah sidrei Mishnah, chamishah chumshei Torah, arba imahot, sh'loshah avot, sh'nei luchot habrit, echad Eloheinu shebashamayim uva'aretz.*

Tishah mi yodei'a? *Tishah ani yodei'a: Tishah yarchei leidah, sh'monah y'mei milah, shivah y'mei shabta, shishah sidrei Mishnah, chamishah chumshei Torah, arba imahot, sh'loshah avot, sh'nei luchot habrit, echad Eloheinu shebashamayim uva'aretz.*

Asarah mi yodei'a? *Asarah ani yodei'a: Asarah dibraya, tishah yarchei leidah, sh'monah y'mei milah, shivah y'mei shabta, shishah sidrei Mishnah, chamishah chumshei Torah, arba imahot, sh'loshah avot, sh'nei luchot habrit, echad Eloheinu shebashamayim uva'aretz.*

Achad asar mi yodei'a? *Achad asar ani yodei'a: Achad asar koch'vaya, asarah dibraya, tishah yarchei leidah, sh'monah y'mei milah, shivah y'mei shabta, shishah sidrei Mishnah, chamishah chumshei Torah, arba imahot, sh'loshah avot, sh'nei luchot habrit, echad Eloheinu shebashamayim uva'aretz.*

Sh'neim asar mi yodei'a? *Sh'neim asar ani yodei'a: Sh'neim asar shivtaya, achad asar koch'vaya, asarah dibraya, tishah yarchei leidah, sh'monah y'mei milah, shivah y'mei shabta, shishah sidrei Mishnah, chamishah chumshei Torah, arba imahot, sh'loshah avot, sh'nei luchot habrit, echad Eloheinu shebashamayim uva'aretz.*

Sh'loshah asar mi yodei'a? *Sh'loshah asar ani yodei'a: Sh'loshah asar midaya, sh'neim asar shivtaya, achad asar koch'vaya, asarah dibraya, tishah yarchei leidah, sh'monah y'mei milah, shivah y'mei shabta, shishah sidrei Mishnah, chamishah chumshei Torah, arba imahot, sh'loshah avot, sh'nei luchot habrit, echad Eloheinu shebashamayim uva'aretz.*

Who knows one? I know one: One is our God in heaven and on earth.

Who knows two? I know two: Two are the tablets of the law, and one is our God in heaven and on earth.

Who knows three? I know three: Three are the patriarchs, two are the tablets of the law, and one is our God in heaven and on earth.

Four are the matriarchs....

Five are the books of the Torah....

Six are the books of the Mishnah....

Seven are the days of the week....

Eight are the days until circumcision....

Nine are the months of pregnancy....

Ten are the commandments....

Eleven are the stars in Joseph's dream....

Twelve are the tribes of Israel....

Thirteen are the attributes of God....

MIND AND BODY

Hold up the appropriate number of fingers each time a number is mentioned in the song and/or create hand motions for each verse.

ENERGY UP!

The rollicking songs that many families end with were originally included to entice the children to stay awake and attentive throughout the seder.

"CHAD GADYA": ONE LITTLE GOAT

Chad gadya, chad gadya, dizvan aba bitrei zuzei, chad gadya, chad gadya.

V'ata shun'ra, v'achlah l'gadya, dizvan aba bitrei zuzei, chad gadya, chad gadya.

V'ata chalba, v'nashach l'shunra, d'achlah l'gadya, dizvan aba bitrei zuzei, chad gadya, chad gadya.

V'ata chutra, v'hikah l'chalba, d'nashach l'shunra, d'achlah l'gadya, dizvan aba bitrei zuzei, chad gadya, chad gadya.

V'ata nura, v'saraf l'chutra, d'hikah l'chalba, d'nashach l'shunra, d'achlah l'gadya, dizvan aba bitrei zuzei, chad gadya, chad gadya.

V'ata maya, v'chavah l'nura, d'saraf l'chutra, d'hikah l'chalba, d'nashach l'shunra, d'achlah l'gadya, dizvan aba bitrei zuzei, chad gadya, chad gadya.

V'ata tora, v'shata l'maya, d'chavah l'nura, d'saraf l'chutra, d'hikah l'chalba, d'nashach l'shunra, d'achlah l'gadya, dizvan aba bitrei zuzei, chad gadya, chad gadya.

V'ata hashocheit, v'shachat l'tora, d'shata l'maya, d'chavah l'nura, d'saraf l'chutra, d'hikah l'chalba, d'nashach l'shunra, d'achlah l'gadya, dizvan aba bitrei zuzei, chad gadya, chad gadya.

V'ata mal'ach hamavet, v'shachat l'shocheit, d'shachat l'tora, d'shata l'maya, d'chavah l'nura, d'saraf l'chutra, d'hikah l'chalba, d'nashach l'shunra, d'achlah l'gadya, dizvan aba bitrei zuzei, chad gadya, chad gadya.

V'ata haKadosh Baruch Hu, v'shachat l'mal'ach hamavet, d'schachat l'shocheit, d'shachat l'tora, d'shata l'maya, d'chavah l'nura, d'saraf l'chutra, d'hikah l'chalba, d'nashach l'shunra, d'achlah l'gadya, dizvan aba bitrei zuzei, chad gadya, chad gadya.

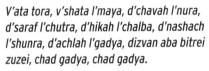

WHO'S WHO IN "CHAD GADYA"

This Aramaic folk song describes Israel's trials with its enemies throughout history. The little goat represents Israel, and the father is God, the Holy One. The two coins, zuzim, are the tablets of the law, and the remaining figures are Israel's past enemies: Assyria (the cat), Babylon (the dog), Persia (the stick), Greece (the fire), Rome (the water), the Saracens (the ox), the Crusaders (the butcher), and the Ottoman Turks (the angel of death).

One little goat, one little goat that my father bought for two *zuzim*, *chad gadya*, *chad gadya*.

Then came a cat and ate the goat my father bought for two *zuzim*, *chad gadya*, *chad gadya*.

Then came a dog and bit the cat that ate the goat my father bought for two *zuzim*, *chad gadya*, *chad gadya*.

Then came a stick and hit the dog that bit the cat that ate the goat my father bought for two *zuzim*, *chad gadya*, *chad gadya*.

Then came a fire and burned the stick that hit the dog that bit the cat that ate the goat my father bought for two *zuzim*, *chad gadya*, *chad gadya*.

Then came water and quenched the fire that burned the stick that hit the dog that bit the cat that ate the goat my father bought for two *zuzim*, *chad gadya*, *chad gadya*.

Then came an ox and drank the water that quenched the fire that burned the stick that hit the dog that bit the cat that ate the goat my father bought for two *zuzim*, *chad gadya*, *chad gadya*.

Then came a butcher and slaughtered the ox that drank the water that quenched the fire that burned the stick that hit the dog that bit the cat that ate the goat my father bought for two *zuzim*, *chad gadya*, *chad gadya*.

Then came the angel of death and killed the butcher that slaughtered the ox that drank the water that quenched the fire that burned the stick that hit the dog that bit the cat that ate the goat my father bought for two *zuzim*, *chad gadya*, *chad gadya*.

Then came the Holy Blessed One and destroyed the angel of death that killed the butcher that slaughtered the ox that drank the water that quenched the fire that burned the stick that hit the dog that bit the cat that ate the goat my father bought for two *zuzim*, *chad gadya*, *chad gadya*.

In every generation we are obligated to show ourselves as if we personally went out of Egypt. Our posture should show the stature of a liberated person. Freedom speaks a special body language reinforcing feeling with actions. On seder night we must act out the past for all to see and to learn.

Adapted from *Mishneh Torah, Chameitz U'matzah* 7:6-7, Moses Maimonides.

MIND AND BODY

Invite seder participants to take roles (goat, cat, dog, etc.) and act out "Chad Gadya" as it is sung.

CONNECTION 📶
TIPS FOR ACTIVELY ENGAGING REMOTE PARTICIPANTS

You can make a memorable seder by including participants who are physically distant. Draw from the ideas below to help ensure that everyone at your seder—whether in person or remote—is fully engaged and can be an active participant.

Appoint a leader or team to organize and facilitate the seder in advance.

- Decide in advance which parts of the seder to include, and annotate your copy of the haggadah to ensure a smooth flow.

- Assign roles to make sure that participants in all locations are included. For example, who will chant the Four Questions, and who will play parts in the "Chad Gadya" song. Plan out reading roles. Make sure each reader is visible to those who are not in the same location.

- Remind participants to prepare in advance. Will each group have its own seder plate? Wine or grape juice, matzah, *maror, charoset*, and salt water? Include any props you will need for active parts of the seder, such as scallions for gently beating each other during Avadim Hayinu.

Make sure each participant has a copy of the haggadah.

Send copies in advance or have participants order copies at www.behrmanhouse.com/seder.

Test any audio- or video-conferencing technology in advance, and ensure that someone at each site is able to help with technical issues.

Think through the best way for attendees to participate: Should everyone be muted, only unmuting themselves when they have a part? Should the facilitator call on guests to unmute themselves? Don't let technology drive the seder; use tech with which you are comfortable. Still, have a backup plan; for example, share phone numbers in case you need to call in.

Make the seder interactive.

Give participants opportunities to contribute throughout.

- Engage children by having them show their own artwork on screen, build an animation of the plagues in advance, or create a house made of matzah. Families can prerecord skits or song parodies.

- Engage seniors by inviting them to show a Passover family heirloom, to briefly describe seders from when they were young, or to lead a movement activity.

- Ask questions for family conversation. Pause so small groups can discuss in their pods. You can also break the large group into smaller rooms if the technology you choose allows; when you are back together, invite a representative of each group to give a recap.

- Look for the *CONNECTION* 📶 feature, located at key points throughout the book, for specific ways to engage participants in multiple locations.

- Use virtual backgrounds; for example, you could put yourself in front of an image of the parting of the Sea of Reeds.

- Intersperse videos and music, remembering to share sound when sharing your screen.

- Capture screenshots or take photos and share them afterward as a memory. Or record the Zoom gathering to go back and enjoy at a later date.

Above all, prepare. That way you will have the peace of mind to find joy in the content and connection of sharing a seder with family and friends both near and far.